Letort Paper

ADAPTING, TRANSFORMING, AND MODERNIZING UNDER FIRE: THE MEXICAN MILITARY 2006-11

Inigo Guevara Moyano

September 2011

FOREWORD

Since President Felipe Calderon took office in December 2006, Mexico has embarked upon the implementation of a culture of law and security that has triggered a war with organized crime. This war has involved all sectors of society and has activated a series of renovations in its armed forces, which to date remain the most trusted institutions in Mexican society.

This groundbreaking Letort Paper is an important contribution to an understanding of the structure, culture, motivators, and challenges of the Mexican military in the 21st century. Mr. Iñigo Guevara Moyano, a Mexican researcher and writer, provides a clear picture of doctrinal and structural transformations, adaptations, and improvement that the Mexican armed forces have endured over the past 5 years. Mr. Moyano focuses on how the counternarcotic role has impacted its organization, deployments, and operations, and how it has generated new doctrinal and equipment requirements. The paper also addresses key areas of national and international concern such as respect for human rights and and the military justice system.

Given Mexico's importance to the United States as its neighbor, ally, and third largest trading partner, understanding the transformation that its armed forces are enduring to assist in the implementation of a culture of law should be of prime concern to all actors—government, private sector, and academia—involved in the decisionmaking process.

DOUGLAS C. LOVELACE, JR.
Director
Strategic Studies Institute

ABOUT THE AUTHOR

INIGO GUEVARA MOYANO is a Mexican writer and analyst specializing in Latin American defense and security issues. He is a former advisor to Mexico's Office of the National Security Council and a former head of statistical analysis at a State-level law enforcement agency in Mexico. Mr. Moyano is a member of the Collective for the Analysis of Security for Democracy (CASEDE), the International Institute for Strategic Studies (IISS), and the Stockholm International Peace Research Institute (SIPRI), where he contributes to the Military Expenditure and Arms Transfer projects. In Washington, DC, he has lectured at the Brookings Institution, Georgetown University, the Center for Strategic and International Studies (CSIS), the State Department's Foreign Service Institute (FSI), Council of the America's (COA), Industrial College of the Armed Forces (ICAF), and Committee on Hemispheric Security of the Organization of American States (OAS). Mr. Moyano's focus is on armed forces' policy, structure, and the procurement of equipment, infrastructure, and technology. Mr. Moyano is the author of *Latin American Fighters* (HARPIA, 2009), a history of jet fighters and armed jet trainers in service with Latin American air arms since 1947, and has published over 50 articles in academic journals and specialized magazines. Mr. Moyano holds a Certification in Administration of Public Security from the Instituto de Administracion Publica de Queretaro (IAPQ), a bachelor's degree in international trade (LIN 00) from the Instituto Tecnologico y de Estudios Superiores de Monterrey (ITESM) in Mexico, a master's degree in international security from Georgetown University, and completed the Strategy and Defense Policy course presented by the Center for Hemispheric Defense Studies (CHDS) at National Defense University.

SUMMARY

Mexico's armed forces are in the midst of a transformation to better perform in an ongoing war against organized crime. Their role and visibility have escalated considerably since President Felipe Calderon assumed office in December of 2006.

Although the fight against organized crime is clearly a law enforcement matter, the absence of effective and accountable police forces has meant that the Army, Navy, and Air Force have been used as supplementary forces to defend the civilian population and enforce the rule of law. While the federal government has striven to stand up a capable police force in order to relieve and eventually replace the military, that possibility is still distant. Five years into the Calderon administration, the armed forces continue to be the main implementers of the National Security policy, aimed at employing the use of force to disrupt the operational capacity of organized crime. Their strong institutional tradition, professionalism, submission to political control, and history of interaction with the population mainly through disaster relief efforts have made them the most trusted institution in Mexican society.

Mexico's armed forces have long been used as an instrument of the state to implement all kinds of public policies at the national level, from emergency vaccinations, to post-earthquake rescue, to reforestation campaigns. They have been at the forefront of disaster relief operations in reaction to the calamities of nature, within and beyond their borders, with humanitarian assistance deployments to Indonesia, the United States, Haiti, and Central America among the most recent.

The Mexican armed forces are quite unique, as they are divided into two separate cabinet-level ministries: the Secretaría de la Defensa Nacional (the Secretary of National Defense or SEDENA), which encompasses the Army and Air Force, and the Secretaría de Marina (the Secretary of the Navy or SEMAR), which comprises the Navy. The level of engagement with society and the results obtained from this division in military power confirms the utility of their independence. Their use as the state's last line of defense has led to severe criticism from opinion leaders, opposition forces, international analysts, and human rights organizations. Their level of commitment remains unaltered and they have undertaken a number of significant transformations to better address their continued roles as the guardians of the State and protectors of the population.

ADAPTING, TRANSFORMING, AND MODERNIZING UNDER FIRE: THE MEXICAN MILITARY 2006-11

Despite considerable attention to and investment in Mexico's law enforcement sector during the past 5 years, the armed forces continue to be the only Mexican institutions with the capabilities to conduct nationwide operations and the main implementers of the government's security policy. This paper analyzes how the counterdrug role has influenced, and in some cases directed, its modernization. It also addresses the main challenges the counterdrug role is associated with, including human rights concerns, and proposes some options for its future.

The Mexican Defense Structure: Roles and Missions.

The fight between state and nonstate groups has characterized warfare in the 21st century; nonstate groups include a wide assortment of terrorists, insurgents, pirates, and criminals. Theaters of operation are as varied as the enemy, ranging from the jungles of Colombia to the mountains of Afghanistan, the coast off Somalia to cyber-space. Urban and suburban settings have generally experienced rapid growth and, with it, the need for governments to provide sufficient services and execute the rule of law.

This variety of threats poses a challenge for security forces, which are generally underfunded and consequently find it difficult to stay ahead of their rapidly evolving enemies. Lack of appropriate police and justice systems generally leads to power vacuums where crime develops. Old and new democracies have turned to their largely cold war militaries to face these new adversaries and, in some cases, provide the only visible presence of the state. Hence, democracies are faced with the problem of not having the appropriate forces to deal with the problem, which in some cases requires good judges and social workers rather than soldiers.

Since the administration of Felipe Calderon assumed office in December 2006, the Mexican armed forces have been the main implementing agents of the country's national security policy, which identifies organized crime, drug trade organizations, and arms trafficking as its priority targets.[1] Mexico possesses a *sui generis* defense establishment composed of two independent institutions: the Ministry of National Defense (SEDENA), which includes the Army and the Air Force (FAM); and the Marine Ministry (SEMAR), comprised of the Navy (ARM), including its general fleet, naval air force, and marine infantry corps. This unique style of organization dates back to 1940, when the Department of the Navy was established as an autonomous entity separate from the Ministry of War. In 1941 the Navy Department received full cabinet ministry status in order to provide it with financial and operational independence to implement the country's maritime policy.[2] The FAM, however, continued to be subordinated to the Army-controlled Ministry of War, which assumed the name of the National Defense Ministry.

The three armed forces are assigned the mission of preserving national security, defined by the Mexican Constitution as defense from external enemies and internal threats.[3] Thus, unlike other armed forces in the hemisphere that are legally barred from projecting power internally, the Mexican Constitution explicitly mandates it. Deployment outside of its borders during peacetime, even to participate in international exercises, requires congressional approval.

The chain of command is simple: the President is commander in chief and has direct control over the armed forces via SEDENA and SEMAR. Each ministry is headed by an active duty four-star general-secretary and admiral-secretary, respectively; the FAM is headed by a three-star general who reports directly to the SEDENA general-secretary.

Both ministries' functions and responsibilities are regulated by the Federal Public Administration Organic Law,[4] with each service having its own organic laws that further specify its roles and missions[5] which are additional to those traditional missions growing out of Mexico's historical and geo-political situation. In general terms, they comprise the defense of the country's sovereignty and territorial integrity, internal security from destabilizing forces, and disaster relief assistance to the population. The Mexican armed forces therefore carry out roles that in other countries are assigned to a variety of civilian agencies and intermediate forces, such as national guards, coast guards, and national police.

There are a number of elite military units, representing all services, directly subordinate to the Office of the President through the Presidential High Command Staff or Estado Mayor Presidencial (EMP). These units include a Presidential Guards Corps, a Marine Infantry Presidential Guard Battalion, and a Presidential Transport Air Group (GATP).[6] The EMP is responsible for the president's personal security. It also acts as a liaison with the military and advises the president on matters of national security. By law, the EMP is headed by an Army general.

Defense Budgeting and Spending.

With the country having no external enemies, funding for the defense sector has been traditionally low. When calculated as a proportion of the country's gross domestic product (GDP), defense expenditures average around 0.5 to 0.7 percent. When compared to other large countries in the hemisphere, Mexico is at the lower end of defense spending.

In the past 5 years the defense budget (including pensions and social services) has gone up 100 percent, but when adjusted for inflation, the real increase has been only slightly over 50 percent (see Figures 1 and 2). As manpower levels increased only by 4 percent from 2006 to 2009 (the last published public figure), most of this increase went to raising salaries and increasing benefits; troops employed in high impact operations received an 80 percent increase between 2006 and 2010. Benefits included the granting of 15,000 housing credits and 35,000 scholarships for military dependents.[7]

	2006	2007	2008	2009	2010	2011
SEDENA	26,032	32,201	34,861	43,623	43,632	50,039
SEMAR	9,163	10,951	13,383	16,059	15,992	18,270
ISSFAM	2,545	2,729	2,998	3,459	4,542	5,852
Total	37,740	45,881	51,242	63,141	64,166	74,161

Source: *Presupuestos de Egresos de la Federacion 2006-2011* published by the Secretaria de Hacienda y Crédito Publico.[8]

Figure 1. Budgets Assigned to Defense Institutions in Millions of Mexican Pesos (MXN).

	2007	2008	2009	2010	2011
Nominal Increase %	21.6%	11.7%	23.2%	1.6%	15.6%
INPC previous year (PY)	4.1%	3.8%	6.5%	3.6%	4.3%
Increase after PY INPC	17.5%	7.9%	16.7%	-1.9%	11.3%

Source: Elaborated by author based on INPC (inflation) figures consulted in the Banco de Mexico inflation portal on December 30, 2010, data for 2010 is as of November 30.[9]

Figure 2. Proportional Changes
to the Defense Budget and Inflation.

Interservice Rivalries and the Competition for Resources.

Despite the administrative division in the services, which guarantees the individual development of the naval and land forces, the armed forces are not immune to the normal interservice rivalries that usually dictate competition for additional resources, especially when it comes to role and mission overlap.

- In February 2007, the SEMAR Commission in Congress petitioned the President to transfer the Army's five Amphibious Special Forces Groups (GANFES) to ARM—along with its financial resources—in order to expand the Navy's Marines.[10] The petition was not accommodated. GANFES remains under SEDENA control, with its five groups stationed in Baja California, Baja California Sur, Sonora, Quintana Roo, and Yucatan, respectively.
- In June 2007, a SEMAR plan to stand up a total of 30 marine infantry battalions (BIM) report-

edly caused antagonism within SEDENA sectors that see their traditional areas of operation co-opted by the Navy's growing land-based component. [11]

- Plans by SEMAR to acquire six *Sukhoi* Su-27 jet fighters from Russia were cancelled, with the existence of the plans later denied in an official SEMAR communiqué in 2007.[12] This change in requirement was attributed to a redesign in the ARM's power projection capabilities by the incoming 2006-12 SEMAR administration. Acquisition of these 4.5 generation fighters would have put the SEMAR-controlled naval air force's (FAN) combat capabilities above those of the Air Force. The Air Force is equipped with third generation *Northrop* F-5E/F *Tiger II* fighters acquired in 1981.

Despite this obvious competition for resources, the proportion of the defense budget assigned to each institution has not varied considerably during the past 5 years (see Figure 3).

Proportion	2006	2007	2008	2009	2010	2011
SEDENA	69%	70%	68%	69%	68%	67%
SEMAR	24%	24%	26%	25%	25%	25%
ISSFAM	7%	6%	6%	5%	7%	8%

Source: Elaborated by author based on *Presupuestos de Egresos de la Federacion 2006-2011.*

Figure 3. Proportional Allocation of Financial Resources to Defense Institutions.

Funding for the interservice social security institution ISSFAM, which addresses healthcare, life insurance, and other services for members of the armed forces and their dependents, has received the largest increase in real terms. This sort of joint institution is a good example of the efficiencies obtained from centralizing supporting services.

Evolution of the Army.

The Army is composed of some 200,000 personnel. The last public document detailing SEDENA personnel composition by ranks shows an 80/20 mix of enlisted and officers, with 537 generals.[13]

The country is divided into 12 Military Regions (RM), each subdivided into a variable number of Military Zones (ZM). ZMs are created according to operational requirements; as of December 2010, there were 46 ZMs.[14] Each zone has a variable number of units assigned. As of February 2011, there are 104 infantry battalions, 24 motorized cavalry regiments, 9 armored reconnaissance regiments, 8 mechanized regiments, 12 Special Forces battalions, 10 military police battalions, 4 engineer battalions, 1 logistics battalion, 3 airborne rifle battalions, 9 artillery regiments, 8 recoilless rifle groups, and 25 independent infantry companies (CINE).[15]

This type of territorial deployment follows a pattern established in 1924 shortly after the end of the Mexican revolution and remains the most viable form of accomplishing the Army's three main missions. The strategic rationale for this type of deployment is the felt need for a "blanket of forces" that provides a multi-layer defense system against a hypothetically larger and superior invading force. The forces would execute light infantry and guerrilla-type operations in order to defeat the invader through attrition. The Army's presence in every major population center, and in some of the most remote places in the country, allows the Army to have a real time power projection capability to counter an insurrection.

Since most of the second half of the 20th century was relatively peaceful, Army forces also took on additional responsibilities regarding the population and the environment. From 1966, the Army began implementing disaster relief operations as part of its mission portfolio and participated in national vaccination, literacy, nutrition, and reforestation campaigns, which created a strong bond between the civilian population and the military. In isolated areas, the Army provided the only state presence.

Adapting the Land Forces.

As part of the SEDENA *2007-2012 Directive for Integrated Combat against Narco-trafficking*, the high command decided to implement the *Centralized planning and decentralized execution* scheme, providing region and zone commanders the operational autonomy needed in order to conceive, plan, and execute high impact operations.[16] The SEDENA high command also issued the *General Directive for Army Training 2007-2012*, which is designed to identify potential leaders and develop leadership qualities, as well as to increase the level of training effectiveness.[17] This new training program is divided into five phases: individual combat, small team, battalion, large unit (brigade level) combined arms, and large forces air-land joint operations. The last two phases, pertinent to conventional warfare operations, will not be implemented during the current administration, making it clear that there is no need at the moment for conventional military training.[18] The initial three phases reflect a heavy emphasis on urban operations, establishing roadblocks, conducting patrols inside and around small towns, and restoring public law and order.[19] These are the types of operations that the Army has been active in throughout the country.

Initiatives to create separate, specialized forces that would focus on the counterdrug role have not prospered. In May 2007 SEDENA announced the establishment of a 10,000-strong Federal Support Forces Corps (CFAF) especially trained and equipped to fight organized crime. This force would be under the direct orders of the President. The initiative faced strong opposition in Congress, where its funding for 2008 was cut off amid concerns that it could mutate into a Praetorian Guard used for political purposes.[20] The initiative was then redrafted and presented in 2009 as a 5,000-strong force under direct orders of the SEDENA General-Secretary. Mexico's Congress also turned thumbs-down on the budget for this initiative.[21]

The Human Rights Component: Complaints vs. Violations.

The prospect of military forces operating in urban settings, especially residential areas, is disturbing to most citizens in the Western Hemisphere. Although it is a valid concern, some human rights-oriented think tanks and advocacy groups have inaccurately portrayed human rights as being violated by the mere presence of soldiers in the streets. The news media have picked up on some of these studies, mostly as headlines without any sort of analytical depth, but propagating the perception that the Mexican Army was engaged in systematic human rights violations.

This perception stems from the fact that the increase in Army deployments to urban areas since December 2006 has occurred in tandem with a rise in complaints filed before the National Human Rights Center (CNDH). These complaints, however, do not constitute violations (see Figure 4).

Status	2006 [22]	2007	2008	2009	2010	Total
Total Filed Complaints	8	376	1,143	1,644	1,320	4,491
Pending from processing	-	-	10	32	369	411
Processed	8	376	1,133	1,612	951	4,080
Recommendations issued by the CNDH	-	7	14	30	22	73
Proportion of recommendation vs complaints	0.0%	1.9%	1.2%	1.8%	1.7%	1.6%

Source: Elaborated by author based on SEDENA and CNDH reports, accessed on January 26, 2011.

Figure 4. Number of Complaints, Status, and Recommendations.

Over half the complaints filed are not related to human rights violations; they are related to electoral, labor, agrarian, environmental, or constitutional interpretation issues (see Figure 5). But by law, all complaints presented at the CNDH have to be filed and processed.

Not related to Human Rights Violations	2,347	58%
Lack of evidence of a Human Rights Violation	1,125	28%
Complainant desisted	236	6%
Conciliated (solved)	107	3%
Integrated into existing investigations (repeat or coincidental complaints)	78	2%
Accepted and transformed into recommendation	73	2%
Complaint was resolved during the process	46	1%
CNDH was not the appropriate agency for the complaint	33	1%
Complainant lacked interest in pursuing the complaint	33	1%
Sent to the corresponding authority	2	0%
Processed complaints	4,080	100%

Figure 5. Resolution of Complaints Processed by CNDH from 2006-10.

Out of the 73 recommendations (on cases that refer to actual human rights violations) issued by the CNDH, all were accepted by SEDENA as of January 2011. Of these 73 recommendations, 14 are identified by SEDENA as being of an internal "administrative nature,"referring to military personnel or their survivors who filed a compliant against SEDENA due to cases of medical malpractice by military healthcare personnel. The other 59 recommendations are directly linked to the Army's operations against organized crime. Of these 59 recommendations, 21 refer to citizens that reported an abuse of power by Army personnel, most of them at roadblocks, but where no physical injury occurred; a further three refer to drivers who failed to stop at Army roadblocks and were fired upon, one of which was reported to be driving while heavily intoxicated. Three more cases relate to civilians who were killed in cross fires, while the remaining 32 recommendations refer to cases of injury, disappearance, torture, and homicide caused by military personnel. Military justice personnel reportedly have investigated 217 of its personnel and as of January 2011, found 39 guilty as charged.

The concept of having civilian courts rule over military-caused abuses is a positive concept when there is a strong and proven judicial system in place. In the case of Mexico, that is not currently the situation. The entire justice system is undergoing what can only be described as a complete overhaul as it morphs from an inquisitorial to an accusatorial system. According to Article 13 of the Mexican Constitution and Articles 57-58 of the Military Code of Justice, the military judicial system has jurisdiction over crimes committed by active duty military personnel against civilians. All other cases are handled by the civilian justice system.[23]

With over 200,000 personnel, the Mexican Army is certainly not immune to the presence of criminal elements within its ranks. To address this liability, SEDENA outlined the need for further professionalization through a doctrine that requires strict adherence to human rights and the rule of law; this need led to the creation in 2008 of the position of General Director for Human Rights in the SEDENA Command structure, a milestone that passed relatively unnoticed by most media and analysts. It is a position designed to promote and strengthen the practice and protection of human rights within the Army's ranks, as SEDENA envisions continuing internal security operations in the long term.[24]

SEDENA acknowledges that as a consequence of its actions against organized crime, criminals, and/or common citizens associated with criminals file false complaints in order to discredit the armed forces.[25]

A number of nongovernmental organizations (NGOs) and think tanks have relied on the larger, unprocessed human rights complaint figure to produce public reports. The repercussion of these reports on the perception of trust in the armed forces was grave, but momentary (See Figure 6, Year 2008). Motivation for these inflammatory reports, beyond a perception of criminal association, lies in the NGOs' need to access funding from national and international government grants, foundations, and private individuals. The U.S.-funded Merida Initiative alone allocated U.S.$61.5 million in FY 2008-10 to programs involving organized civil society.[26]

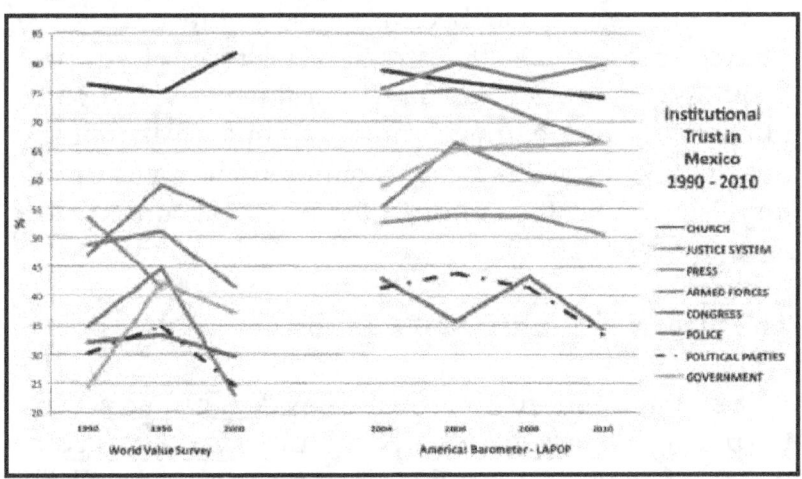

Source: LAPOP 2010 from Bailey *et al.*, "Army as Police? Correlates of Public Confidence in the Police, Justice System, and the Military: Mexico in Comparative Context," January 28, 2011.

Figure 6. Institutional Trust in Mexico 2004-10.

A Wake Up Call.

As SEDENA modified its doctrine, training, and deployment to better adapt to long-term internal security operations, it created permanent community liaison offices that would work to minimize the impact of its operations on society. In June 2010, SEDENA created the Civil–Military Liaison Unit (UNIVIC), with the mission to strengthen communication and foment constructive links between SEDENA and civil society. It is designed to solve problems and minimize the negative effects of the prolonged presence of troops in the streets.[27] Civilians with experience in public policy, human rights, and the Culture of Peace have been invited to form part of this unit. During the 2 months of operations before the SEDENA 2009-10 report was published, UNIVIC resolved five cases in which people had been adversely affected by the Army's presence in the streets. The type of support provided includes covering funeral expenses, reparations, medical treatment, and psychological therapy for victims. As of 2010, the trust perception of the military is back on top among Mexican institutions (see Figure 6, Year 2010).

The Need for Additional Manpower.

Several attempts to reform Mexico's public security (police) system, which by December 2010 was composed of over 2,040 police departments and 447,922 personnel at the municipal, state, and federal levels, have not progressed. The 2010 initiative to create 32 state police forces that would absorb the roles and functions of the municipal forces, creating more resilient, accountable, and efficient forces, was held up in

Congress, with debate delayed until the first term of 2011. Even with this large police enforcement reform in place, the Unified Police Command will face an enormous challenge of acquiring credible capabilities over the next few years. Its focus will be on general public crime, rather than organized crime.

The Federal Police has grown from 6,500 agents in December 2006 to 35,500 by December 2010,[28] but still lacks the technical capability, infrastructure, and numbers to provide a permanent nation-wide presence. Expanding it continues to be a priority, but expansion needs to be performed at a slower pace; training professional police officers should not be rushed.

The Army remains the only institution with the infrastructure and capabilities to stabilize large regions that come under intense criminal cartel violence. As the violence expands or shifts, additional forces are needed to secure areas where the state has historically neglected to establish its presence. Army troops cannot substitute for police in conducting day-to-day law enforcement activities, but they can provide security umbrellas in towns that are under siege by gangs of armed men. Latin American countries that use their armed forces for similar internal security, infrastructure protection, and national development roles have forces—military and paramilitary—that proportionately far exceed those of Mexico (See Figure 7).

	Colombia	Venezuela	Bolivia	Peru	Mexico
Population	43,677,372	26,814,843	9,775,246	29,546,963	111,211,789
Military	285,220	163,000	46,100	114,000	267,506
Paramilitary	144,097	36,000	37,100	77,000	36,400
Total Security Forces	429,317	199,000	83,200	191,000	303,906
Military per 100K	653.0	607.9	471.6	385.8	240.5
Intermediate Forces per 100K	329.9	134.3	379.5	260.6	32.7
SF per 100K	982.9	742.1	851.1	646.4	273.3

Source: elaborated by author based on figures in IISS *The Military Balance 2010*, the International Institute for Strategic Studies; Venezuelan figures are based on the author's research from official Venezuelan sources.

Figure 7. Population, Active Military, and Paramilitary Forces, 2010.

Raising forces to a level comparable to that of these countries would need to see the Mexican military expand by a number in the range of 160,000-460,000, with the bulk of it destined for the Army. Intermediate forces would also need to be expanded in the 110,000-330,000 range.

Tackling Desertion.

Desertion in the Army has long been an issue. From 2000 to 2005, a total of 106,814 members of the Army deserted (17,802 per year on average).[29] Retaining skilled troops became a priority for the new administration, and President Calderon announced in February 2007 that pay would increase by 46 percent for enlisted personnel.[30] Additionally, recruiters began in 2008 to refine their promotion criteria, launching a program to identify and promote leadership qualities among the ranks. In February 2009, President Calderon announced another 40 percent budget increase for enlisted personnel to be applied to pay and benefits.[31]

As part of a morale-boosting effort, SEDENA reinstated a directive providing military honors for troops killed in high impact operations, consisting of a 21-gun salute burial, military band, and memorial flag, accompanied by a life pension for their dependents. The programs had an immediate beneficial effect on the number of desertions recorded from 2008 (see Figure 8).

	2006	2007	2008	2009	2010
Desertions	16,405	16,641	9,112	6,879	2,986

Source: SEDENA Response to a Federal Institute of Access to Information (IFAI) information request, file 0000700020310, and October 2010, p. 7.

Figure 8. Number of SEDENA desertions recorded 2006-10.[32]

Conscription Not a Viable Option.

The objective of the National Military Service (*Servicio Militar Nacional, or SMN*) is twofold: first, to develop values and virtues to strengthen the self-identify of the conscripts as Mexicans; and second, to form a cadre of reserves that are trained and available to satisfy the mobilization requirements in case of external war or the serious disruption of public peace and internal order.[33] During the summer of 2009, the Army launched a pilot program using 330 conscripts to perform drug eradication duties in Michoacán. The unit was led by active duty officers, and conscripts were equipped and armed to the same standards as professional troops. They received a stipend equaling that of a private's pay for the duration of their service. Once their tour was finished, they were excused from the year-long weekend drills. They eradicated illegal crops of 190 plantations from June 26 to July 28, 2009, and then went on to participate in a program in which they toured several public schools, sharing their experiences over the summer and promoting a culture of lawfulness.[34]

Provisional military service in Mexico is compulsory for all males that turn 18. They must all register for service, but only about 10 percent of the total have to take the program itself, consisting of Saturday-only drills, literacy campaigns, and public works. Females may volunteer to participate in the program; their participation has increased from 1,856 volunteers in 2008 to 4,152 in 2009.

In case of a mobilization, conscripts would reinforce battalions and regiments by 300 personnel each, and CINE and artillery groups by 100 each. In 2010 the number of conscripts inducted for the weekend program was 83,192 from a possible total of 835,440.[35] However, modifying the terms of service to embrace genuine full-time conscription is not an option, as it would lead to high desertion rates and likely pose a negative impact on society. Army recruitment continues to be directed at potential candidates for a military career.

In October 2010, the SEDENA Commission in Congress promoted an initiative to fund the creation of 10,000 new slots that would allow for the establishment of 18 new infantry battalions.[36] These new battalions, to be created from the expansion of CINE, would be fully operational by the end of 2011. The requested MXN 13 billion pesos (U.S.$1.08 billion) was turned down by Congress when it approved the 2011 budget in December 2010.[37] As of March 2011, the expansion initiative continued to be debated by members of the National Defense Commission in Congress.

The Combat Inventory.

Conventional capabilities are very limited compared to other forces in Latin America. Since 2004, the Army has not acquired a single piece of military hardware considered to be within the conventional arms category.[38]

Armor holdings include 985 vehicles, most of them obsolete. Some 28 percent of them were built in the 1980s, another 15 percent were built in the 1970s, and the rest were built in the 1940s to 1960s. Since the late 1990s, there has been a modernization effort in place based on standardizing key components, such as weapons and engines, in order to streamline maintenance and logistics. This program has resulted in a number of 1950s and 1960s vehicles, such as the M8 Greyhound armored car and the AMX-VCI mechanized infantry vehicle, being almost completely rebuilt and redesigned. Local production of soft skinned vehicles known as the DN-series, which took place during the 1980s with the participation of local vehicle manufacturer DINA and the Army's military industries, has not resumed.

There are no heavy or medium artillery pieces in service. Artillery regiments are equipped with M101, M2A1, M3, and Italian OTO Melara M56 pack howitzers. The last known acquisition of artillery took place in 2004, when 13 NORINCO M90 105 mm howitzers were procured from China. Being a predominantly infantry force, the Army assures that mortar assets are abundant, including some developed indigenously in the 60 mm and 120 mm range. There are only a handful of anti-tank missiles of an early generation (Milan wire-guided), and the Army has no organic air defense capability.

The Army is equipped only for low-intensity conflict, for which infantry weapons have assumed overriding importance in the past decade. The SEDENA-run Military Factories in Mexico City produced the Heckler und Koch family of small arms and light weapons under license, and have begun production of an indigenous assault rifle—the FX-05 Xiuhcóatl, a North Atlantic Treaty Organization (NATO) standard 5.56 mm assault rifle especially designed by the Military Factories. SEDENA is transitioning from the 7.62 mm G-3 to the smaller and more efficient caliber.

Unit-level communication systems were also in need of replacement by 2009, with close to 90 percent of the Army's radio communication equipment considered obsolete.[39] The Army began receiving a new generation of Harris Falcon II radios starting in 2008. Other major procurement programs during the past 4 years have centered on the establishment of a complete Command, Control, Communications, Computers, Intelligence, Surveillance, and Reconnaissance (C4ISR) network, linking Military Regions, Military Zones, and units down to battalion level.

Anti-Narco Influence on Procurement.

The most representative example of how the anti-narcotic role has influenced Mexican military procurement is the 2008 decision to acquire 4x4 pickup trucks over a 2006 stated requirement for 1,000 High Mobility Multi-purpose Wheeled Vehicles (aka Humvees [HMMWVs] or Hummers). Under [program 9071100001] *the Acquisition of Light Vehicles for Personnel Transport,* the Army sought 1,640 4x4 pickup trucks and 360 double cab 4x4 pickup trucks in order to *provide operational units with vehicles that have the adequate speed and characteristics for operations in support of public security forces against organized crime within the national territory.*[40] General Motors was the selected supplier, and the 2,000 pickup trucks were upgraded by the Army's workshops by adding a roll bar, reinforced bumper, hooks, and armament bed to make them suitable for military urban operations.

HMMWVs were still being acquired, but in smaller quantities; in 2009 the Army received 254 HMMWVs, and in February 2010 it ordered another 200.[41] In February 2011, the Mexican Army announced that it would begin assembling the Oshkosh SandCat protected patrol vehicle at its Military Factories. The SandCat is part of a new generation of 4x4 vehicles designed for the 21st century battlefield, with additional armor protection for its crew and the speed and agility of a truck. It is based on a commercial Ford F-550 chassis and is classed in the Protected Patrol Vehicle (PPV) category.

While pickup trucks, Humvees, and new PPVs provide land mobility, the Army is implementing new technology to help its troops detect the presence of illegal substances, be they drugs, explosives, or weapons, through nonintrusive detection systems. As of February 2011, the Army operated 739 GT-200-18 Buster contraband detector kits and 43 GE Mobile Trace devices used to detect drugs and other illicit contraband, primarily onboard commercial containers and vehicles.[42]

A final example is the MXN 1.7 billion (U.S.$140 million) program to build 13 Strategic Control Posts (PPCCEE) designed to inspect vehicles to detect narcotics, weapons, and other illegal goods. The PPCCEEs will be located in Baja California, Chihuahua, Nuevo Leon, Oaxaca, Sinaloa, Sonora, and Tamaulipas.[43]

The Mexican Air Force Command.

The FAM headquarters is located across the street from the SEDENA building in Mexico City; in 2006 FAM was a very centralized service with about 35 percent of its total assets concentrated at a single base a few miles north of Mexico City. Following the SEDENA's decentralization initiative and in accordance with the *Directiva para el Combate Integral al Narcotráfico 2007-2012*, aircraft and helicopters have been deployed and assigned directly to the regional commanders.[44]

The FAM provides a clear example of an air arm almost entirely devoted to the anti-narcotic role; during the 2006-11 time frame, it has received or placed on order 80 aircraft and helicopters, eight of which have been funded by the United States through the Merida Initiative.[45] Some 96 percent of these assets — including transport aircraft — have been acquired with counterdrug and organized crime as their stated primary or secondary roles, with training focused accordingly. The FAM has established specialized spraying and field-spotting training centers.

FAM aircraft, equipment, procedures, technology, and capabilities have evolved over the years, but its organizational structure remains basically unchanged from post-World War II, when it included a single fighter squadron, half a dozen close-air support (CAS) squadrons, a reconnaissance unit, a transport wing equipped with heavy and medium transport aircraft, and some liaison units.

Despite this World War II era structure, the FAM has not been immune to the global trend of introducing Unmanned Aerial Vehicle (UAV) operations. On April 30, 2009, it began operating an unknown number of Elbit Hermes 450 systems, and up to July 2010 their performance was rated as satisfactory by SEDENA.[46]

Electronic intelligence, signals intelligence, and airborne early warning operations are provided by an EMBRAER EMB-145MP patrol aircraft and an EMB-145SA airborne early warning (AEW) craft, and four C-26B Metro tracker aircraft that make up the aerial detection component of the country's Integrated Air Surveillance System (SIVA). SIVA, designed by SEDENA with the participation of private entities, comprises a collection of assets including air- and land-based radars. Its purpose is to detect suspicious or illegal flights and coordinate the air, sea, or land assets needed to intercept.

Increasing the processing capabilities of the SIVA Command Center (CMCSIVA), expanding radar coverage, and replacing the obsolete Westinghouse TPS-70 3-D radars are current priorities. Two additional EMB-145SA AEW aircraft are required to provide adequate surveillance along the southern border.[47]

Transport aviation has received some attention, including the acquisition of five C-295M medium transports from Airbus Military to replace the *Antonov* An-32B transports in the 301st Squadron, and procurement was announced of an additional five Lockheed C-130 *Hercules* heavy transports to complement the 302nd Squadron. The C-295M acquisition is of particular note, as it comprised the first use of leasing as a procurement method. Under this scheme, state-owned BANOBRAS public works bank acquired the aircraft and leased them to the FAM over a 20-year period.

The transport helicopter fleet comprised some 44 medium lift helicopters consisting of a mix of *Sikorsky* CH-53, UH-60L *Black Hawks*, Mi-8, Mi-17s, and AS-332 *Super Pumas*, plus 14 of the smaller *Bell* 212s and 4 of the *Bell* 412s. Expansion of the fleet has not been a priority. The U.S. Government supplied eight *Bell* 412EPs from December 2009 to December 2010 as part of the Merida Initiative to enhance the mobility of Mexico's forces, and the FAM ordered 12 EC725 medium helicopters in 2009 and 2010 through two separate contracts, with deliveries scheduled to begin in 2011. However, both types will replace older retiring *Bell* 212s and Mi-17s. The up-to-date technology of the new acquisitions will lower operational costs. The second batch of the EC725s was also underwritten by the leasing method, with BANOBRAS as the principal financial agent. The selection of the EC725 over the UH-60 *Black Hawk* or Mi-17, both types with accomplished service records in the FAM, was facilitated by offset agreements signed between the Mexican government and Eurocopter, an EADS subsidiary, which will invest close to U.S.$550 million in a parts assembly plant in Mexico.[48]

Intensifying the Counterdrug Role.

In February 2007, the FAM absorbed the aerial eradication duties that had previously been assigned to the Attorney General's (PGR) Air Wing, receiving an inventory of 50 *Bell* 206 helicopters configured for aerial spraying, 8 *Cessna* TU206G light aircraft, MXN 50 million for their repair, 175 PGR contract personnel who were hired by the FAM, five primary bases of operation, and five secondary bases of operation.[49] Assimilation of this large package took a little over 3 years, with the FAM also taking responsibility for the training of its personnel as well as providing the required maintenance to the *Bell* 206 fleet. By August 2010, the FAM was operating 42 of the *Bell* 206 helicopters in aerial spraying duties, with the other eight undergoing repairs.[50]

Helicopter crew training has received priority, with the FAM acquiring five flight simulators for the *Bell* 206, *Bell* 412, and MD530s. In December 2010, the FAM sent a group of 24 pilots to receive training at the Colombian Air Force's Helicopter Flying School at Melgar, Colombia.[51]

Prior to the transfer of the PGR's eradication duty, the FAM had already undertaken the heavy brunt of the counterdrug role. Six squadrons equipped with the *Cessna* 182S single engine aircraft were created in the early 2000s, serving as spotter and forward air control (FAC) craft in support of the Army's eradication program. In 2007, the FAM established the Cessna Pilot Training Center *(Centro de Adiestramiento para Pilotos Aviadores de Cessna)* at El Cipres airbase in Baja, California, to specialize in this type of training.[52]

Air Defense Needs Neglected.

Retirement of the legacy *Lockheed* T-33 jet trainers in 2007 has happened without a replacement, leaving air sovereignty patrols and interceptions to a dwindling number of *Pilatus* PC-7 turbo-prop armed trainers or the single squadron of supersonic F-5E *Tiger II* tactical fighters. In 2008 SEDENA sent a request to Congress for procurement of 12 Lockheed-Martin F-16 fighters, which would allow establishment of a second fighter squadron, and four batteries of air defense systems (of an unspecified type). The request was ignored.[53] A proposed avionics update for the ageing F-5E and PC-7 fleets has also been mired in a state of uncertainty. The current national security priorities require at least a two-tier solution that can tackle targets ranging from very slow low-flying ultra lights to supersonic Biz-jets. Air defense, precision strike, close air support, and armed reconnaissance are conventional capabilities that will also need to be addressed eventually.

The Naval Ministry.

The Secretaria de Marina (SEMAR - Ministry of the Navy) and its military service, the Armada de Mexico (ARM - Mexican Navy), have assumed considerably increased profiles by modernizing, transforming, and adapting their forces to be a major partner in the implementation of the government's national security policy. Much like the Army, the ARM's missions are to provide external defense and internal security, guarantee constitutional order (maritime law enforcement), and provide safety to the population in cases of natural disasters and emergencies.[54]

In the 2006-11 time frame, SEMAR reorganized its command structure, rebuilt its marine infantry force, created a naval intelligence agency (UIN), reinforced its naval aviation, and formed a network of coast guard-style stations to enhance SAR and law enforcement presence. Attention to its ocean-going fleet is less notable, as it has specialized in the anti-narcotic and maritime law enforcement roles since the 1980s. From 2007, the sea, land, and air elements of SEMAR have been separated and reorganized within a so-called corps system, comprising a General Fleet Corps, Marine Infantry Corps, and Naval Aeronautics Corps.

Command and Territorial Reorganization.

The previous command structure of the ARM comprised two regional headquarters (HQs), one on each coast, which controlled all surface, air, and land forces assigned to it and reported to SEMAR HQ. This organization was revamped with the regional HQs deleted. A single General HQ is based in Mexico City, overseeing all naval operations. *This command restructure, which follows a political-strategic character, has the specific intention of generating better efficiency in the navy's participation against organized crime and insecurity.*[55]

SEMAR's territorial organization follows a model comprising a Naval Region/Naval Zone/Naval Sector pattern that mirrors the Army's Military Region/Military Zone/Garrison pattern. Each naval region controls a flotilla of varying size. These are separated into destroyer (including destroyers and frigates) and auxiliary flotillas. The seven regions are divided into 13 Naval Zones and 14 Naval Sectors.

The Green Water Fleet.[56]

The main seagoing fleet is spearheaded by four 1970s-vintage *Allende*-class (ex-U.S. Navy *Knox*) frigates delivered between 1997 and 2002. These ships are the most powerful sea going vessels in service and are complemented by two more *Bravo*-class (ex-U.S. *Bronstein*-class) frigates and an ageing *Quetzalcoatl*-class (ex-U.S. *Gearing*) destroyer that dates from World War II. Another World War II-era ship, the destroyer escort *Manuel Azueta* (ex-U.S. *Edsall*), continues in service although it is designated for training; commissioned in 1945 and 1943 respectively, the last two operational destroyers will need to be withdrawn shortly as increased maintenance costs make them burdens. Replacement with destroyer-size ships is unlikely under current budget allocations and requirements. This type of transformation follows a global tendency to shift from the larger power-projection ships to smaller, faster, multi-purpose vessels.

The amphibious warfare fleet is composed of two *Papaloapan*-class (ex-U.S. *Newport*) landing ship-tanks (LST) that were delivered in 2000 and 2001. At 5,200-tons, these are the largest ships in the fleet and have deployed in humanitarian assistance missions to foreign countries including the United States (Hurricane Katrina in 2005), the tsunami in Indonesia (2005), and major storm disasters in Haiti (2008, 2010). They are complemented by a pair of locally designed auxiliary support ships and a single *Panuco* (ex-U.S. LST-1152) which will be replaced soon (it was first commissioned in 1945) by a pair of 3,300-ton logistics support ships being built at Mexican shipyards, with construction having started in January 2010 and delivery expected in 2012-13.[57]

The Patrol Force Fleet comprises 31 ocean patrol vessels (OPV) and over 80 interceptor craft, the majority of which have been built in Mexican shipyards. Indigenous design and development of OPVs started in the late 1980s based on experience with the six *Halcon*-class corvettes acquired from Spain. From that point on, the anti-narcotic and maritime law enforcement role became the driving force in ship design and operational requirements.

The most recent indigenous development is the *Oaxaca*-class OPV, a 1,680-ton vessel, similar in size to a USCG 270-ft medium endurance cutter. It is equipped with an AS-565MB *Panther* helicopter and two fast interceptor crafts, making it an ideal platform for anti-narcotic operations. There are four *Oaxacas* in service and two more under construction; they have been preceded by the 1,554-ton *Durango*-class vessel (delivered 2000-01), 1,200-ton *Sierra*-class (delivered 1999-2000), and 1,290-ton *Holzinger*-class (1991-94). Ten *Auk-class* ex-minesweepers modified as patrol vessels also need to be replaced shortly as these have been in service with the Mexican Navy since 1973, having been originally commissioned in the U.S. Navy between 1942 and 1945.[58]

Since drug trafficking organizations concentrated on the use of fast boats in the late 1980s and 1990s, which could easily outturn and outrun the larger and older OPV and coastal patrol vessels, the ARM adapted. All of its OPVs are helicopter-equipped, either from scratch or as modified with platforms. The use of helicopters to spot and pursue targets at sea developed into the *Trinomio* tactic, which includes the use of an OPV, an air asset, and a fast interceptor craft.

The need for additional fast interceptors was evident, and in 2000 the Mexican Government signed a deal with the Swedish shipyard Dockstavarvet for the procurement of 40 Combat Boat CB90HMN interceptor craft capable of speeds well over 45 knots.[59] The agreement also included assembly of the craft in Mexico with follow-on requirements of at least 100 more of these boats in service. Sixteen were built locally by 2006 before production shifted to the faster *Interceptor* craft IC16M, which has speeds of over 50 knots.[60] The requirement for the 100-interceptor craft fleet was scaled back by the current administration to 17.

Building a Coast Guard Network.

In order to enhance its search and rescue (SAR) capabilities, SEMAR launched the Sistema de Busqueda y Rescate (SAR System) consisting of 17 SAR naval stations (ENSAR) throughout the coastal region. Five of these are categorized as ENSAR-A, comprising two *Safe Boat Defender*-class patrol boats, a Marine *Textron* MLB unsinkable patrol boat, and an MD902 helicopter. The remainder, categorized as ENSAR-B, are equipped with two *Defenders* each. The first ENSAR began operations during April 2007, and 12 were in operation by early 2011. In addition to their stated SAR role, these stations provide an enhanced law enforcement presence.

Marine Corps Revival.

The most demanding task for the current SEMAR administration has been the reestablishment of an adequate marine infantry force. The previous SEMAR administrations halved the 11,000-strong marine force, transferring 5,000 marines to the newly created Federal Preventive Police (PFP) between 1999 and 2006.[61] In December 2006, the then new Secretary of the Navy was instructed to transfer another 2,500 naval personnel to support the PFP. By March 2007, it was clear that naval personnel would not voluntarily transfer to the PFP. The SEMAR leadership therefore offered an alternative to PFP: raise its own military forces that would be capable of implementing the maritime police role.[62]

At the time, the Marine Corps consisted of two amphibious force groups (one on each coast), trained and equipped for amphibious landings, and two marine infantry battalions (one airborne, one presidential guard) based in Mexico City. The challenge was to create a force of 30 marine infantry battalions that would be permanently based in the coastal states and provide internal security (protection of strategic installations; combating traffic of narcotics, people, and weapons; search and rescue; and maritime route security). Manpower allocations for Marine infantry battalions were also raised from a previously depleted level of around 400 to the 650-680 mark, making the Mexican Marine Infantry Corps second in number only to that of the United States. Since the main task to be performed by these 30 battalions was anti-organized crime, the equipment procured for them included logistic vehicles such as pickup trucks and troop carriers, infantry weapons, and communications equipment.

Along with the Marine Corps expansion, a third special forces unit was based in Mexico City during 2008. These special forces are mainly drawn from marines and are being organized into a Marine Infantry Special Operations Brigade, with detachments throughout the country. Their close relationship with the UIN, which itself was formed during 2008, have made them the main reaction forces employed in hunting down cartel leaders, even in land-locked places such as Mexico City, Cuernavaca, and Monterrey. The UIN possesses advanced collection and analytical capabilities and is regarded as the most efficient and collaborative Mexican intelligence agency by foreign intelligence services.

Transformation of Naval Aviation Requirements.

A radical shift in naval aviation planning saw the decision to exchange a requirement for 12 jet fighters to a requirement for a fleet of 15 turbo-prop maritime surveillance aircraft. SEMAR, which already possessed eight C-212PM maritime patrol aircraft, selected the CN-235MP offered by EADS-CASA (now known as Airbus Military). Commonality with the C-212 (also an Airbus Military product) and with the U.S. Coast Guard's HC-144 ocean sentry (the USCG designation of its CN-235MPs) was a factor. The SEMAR and USCG versions are not identical, differing in their mission control packages.

Air transport requirements for naval aviation foresee an increase from the capability to ferry 5,816 troops and 224 tons of cargo in 2009, to 19,252 and 1,197 tons by 2012. This will require increasing the transport aircraft fleet from 6 to 17.[63] So far, four C-295M medium transports have been acquired to complement the four Ukrainian-built An-32B medium transports procured in the mid 1990s. The last two C-295Ms were acquired through a leasing agreement with state development bank BANOBRAS. The acquisition of these aircraft was justified on the same basis: increased efficiency in aeronautical operations in military transport and cargo activities such as protecting human life at sea; combating illegal traffic of narcotics, people, and weapons; and assisting the population in case of disasters and emergencies.[64]

The ARM has also pioneered the use of indigenous unmanned aerial systems (UAS). Furthermore, the SEMAR research and development institute began its own UAS project during 2010. The first UAS unit was to have been set up in 2010 with the indigenously developed S4 *Ehectal* (God of the Wind) tactical UAV, E1 *Gavilan* mini-UAV, and mobile ground control centers in the state of Tamaulipas.[65] Its implementation appears to have been delayed, but the beginning of UAS operations in support of marine counternarcotic operations is imminent.

Naval Procurement, Assistance, and Cooperation.

Over the 2006-11 period, the Navy has received over U.S.$ 808 million worth of equipment comprising four *Oaxaca*-class ocean patrol vessels, nine IC16M interceptor craft (known as *Polaris II*), 34 Safe Boat Defender coastal patrol boats, and six unsinkable Textron MLB motor life boats; aviation assets have included three AS-565MB *Panther* multi-mission helicopters, one *Kazan* Mi-17V-5 medium-lift helicopter, one S4 *Ehectal* UAS, four CN-235MP maritime patrol aircraft, four C-295M medium transport aircraft, and one *Gulfstream* VIP aircraft; and land vehicles, mainly for the marines, have included 164 Unimog 4000 troop carriers, 84 Mercedes G-class and 22 Land Rover Defender 130 light armored vehicles.

During the same period, the United States has announced transfers of four additional CN-235MP *Persuader* maritime patrol aircraft worth U.S.$210 million; and three UH-60M *Black Hawk* medium-lift helicopters worth U.S. $71 million. No deliveries of any of these were reported as of February 2011.

Conclusion.

The campaign against organized crime, particularly narco-trafficking and arms smuggling, has been the main driver in the modernization of Mexico's armed forces. The need to rely on the armed forces as the lead instrument in implementing the national security policy is a reflection of historical neglect, which long precedes the current administration, of developing capable and democratic law enforcement institutions. Although federal police institutions have been considerably expanded in manpower and capabilities during the past 5 years, they still lack the institutional depth—experience and continuity—to take on a principal role.

The main challenges to the Mexican military in the 21st century will be:

- To remain an apolitical force, which currently can be achieved only by being directly subordinate to the executive and increasingly accountable through the legislature to the bicameral Commission on National Security, as well as the National Defense and Navy Commissions.
- To continue to be a purely professional and volunteer-based force, striving towards specialization by forming dedicated agencies and mission-specific units.
- To prioritize respect of human rights and the rule of law in order to maintain the military's legitimacy. This priority needs not only to be clarified, but to be communicated, both domestically and abroad.
- To remain a credible defense force by assimilating new technology and specializing so as to address the changing nature of threats. Cyber defense, information operations, and underwater warfare are also areas currently in need of attention. Finally, airpower needs to be modernized and expanded considerably, especially regarding air mobility, ISR, and sovereignty control capabilities.
- To cooperate and coordinate (C&C) with national and international agencies—military and civilian. C&C needs to be mission- or purpose-specific, with specifically defined boundaries and responsibilities. C&C needs to be expand-

ed and enhanced considerably, especially with the main partners in the area: the United States, Guatemala, Belize, Colombia, El Salvador, and Honduras.

- To strengthen defense diplomacy. C&C requires effective negotiation by the corresponding diplomatic authorities. Participation in international peacekeeping and humanitarian relief operations—be they regional, multilateral, or binational—is entirely a political decision. The military, however, needs to be involved in the decisionmaking process to assure that the proper capabilities are in place to implement said policy.

- To create a civilian career service. The Mexican armed forces, despite nominal increases in salaries and benefits over the past 5 years, remain considerably underfunded and undermanned. Opening up civil service careers would lessen the strain on manpower resources as well as the cost of militarizing all members of the defense institutions. This would make the institutions more efficient and help provide a precedent and model on how to implement a professional career service in Mexican Government institutions. The professional career path is currently present only in the armed forces and foreign service.

Counterdrug and law enforcement operations ideally should be performed by capable and accountable civilian institutions. However, these are not yet in place. Institutions and communities need to be strengthened at the economic, judicial, educational, and cultural levels. These deep transformations will require decades of effort before they produce measurable effects. As of 2011, the Mexican armed forces remain the most valued and trusted forces in place to implement the national security policy, and to provide models for the type of stable and long-term institutions Mexico requires.

ENDNOTES

1. *Programa para la Seguridad Nacional 2009-2012* (*National Security Program 2009-2012*), Mexico City, Mexico: Office of the President, p. 2.

2. Department of Historical Research, Veracruz Naval Museum, Creation of the Autonomous Department and the Ministry of the Navy, available from *www.cesnav.edu.mx/foro_new/Historia/ siglo_xx/pdf/Departamento_Autonomo.pdf.*

3. *Idem.*

4. *Organic Law of the Federal Public Administration*, Arts. 29 and 30.

5. For more on this, see Organic Law of the Mexican Navy, December 30, 2002; and Organic Law of the Army and Air Force, December 26, 1986.

6. Regulation of the Presidential High Command Staff, available from *www.presidencia.gob.mx/estadomayor/.*

7. Presidency of the Republic, Dialogues on the 4th year of government, p. 11.

8. Available from *www.apartados.hacienda.gob.mx/presupuesto/ index.html.*

9. Available from *www.banxico.org.mx/portal-inflacion/index. html.*

10. Jorge Luis Sierra, "Duplicidad en las fuerzas armadas" ("Duplicity in the armed forces"), El Universal, February 27, 2007, available from *www.eluniversal.com.mx/editoriales/36895.html*.

11. Carrillo Olea, "Jorge in La guerra entre Ejército y Marina por el poder"("The war between the army and the navy for power"), *La Jornada*, August 26, 2010, available from *www.jornada. unam.mx/2010/08/26/index.php?section=opinion&article=016a1pol*.

12. Ministry of the Navy press release, 015/2007.

13. Available from *www.apartados.hacienda.gob.mx/presupuesto/ temas/pef/2009/temas/tomos/07/r07_app.pdf*.

14. Ministry of National Defense, Reglamento General de Regiones y Zonas Militares (Ministry of National Defense, General Regulation on Military Regions and Zones), Art. 8.

15. Ministry of National Defense website; and author's databases.

16. Ministry of National Defense, Cuarto Informe de Labores (Ministry of National Defense), *Fourth Annual Report 2006-2012*, p. 116.

17. *Ibid.; Directiva General de Adiestramiento del Ejército y Fuerza Aérea Mexicanos 2007-2012 (experimental)* (*General Training Directive of the Mexican Army and Air Force 2007-2012 [experimental]*).

18. Ministry of National Defense, Cuarto Informe de Labores (Ministry of National Defense), *Fourth Annual Report 2006-2012*, p. 41.

19. *Ibid.*

20. Jesus Aranda, "Riesgo de que el cuerpo de fuerza especial se use para reprimir: experto" ("Risk that the Special Force will be used to repress: expert"), *Jornada*, September 20, 2007, available from *www.jornada.unam.mx/2007/09/20/index.php?section=politica& article=016n1pol*.

21. Benito Jiménez, "Frenan legisladores grupo elite de Ministry of National Defense" ("Legislators freeze Ministry of National Defense elite group"), *Reforma*, August 29, 2009.

22. Only December 2006.

23. U.S. Department of State, Mexico-Merida Initiative report on Human Rights, August 2009.

24. Ministry of National Defense, *Second Annual Report (2007-2008)*.

25. Ministry of National Defense, *Quejas y recomendaciones (Human Rights Complaints and Recommendations)*, available from *www.sedena.gob.mx/images/stories/archivos/derechos_humanos/ quejasyrecom/SITUACIN_DE_QUEJAS_Y_RECOMENDACIO-NES._ENERO.pdf*.

26. As part of the Merida Initiative, the U.S. Government designated U.S.$61.5 million in FY2008-10 for programs involving organized civil society.

27. Ministry of National Defense, *Fourth Annual Report (2006-2012)*, p. 57.

28. Alejandro Poire, presentation at Georgetown University, February 2, 2011.

29. Ministry of National Defense, request for information dated November 30, 2009; file 0000700168009.

30. Miriam Castillo, "Aumentan hasta 46% salarios en el Ejercito" ("Army salaries increase up to 46%"), *La Cronica*, February 20, 2007, available from *www.cronica.com.mx/nota.php?id_ nota=286803*.

31. Ramos P. Fernando, "FCH anuncia aumento de salario a tropas" ("FCH increases troop wages"), *El Universal*, February 19, 2010, available from *www.eluniversal.com.mx/notas/660052.html*.

32. Data for 2010 are as of September; annual projection would be 3,981.

33. Ministry of National Defense, Definition on Servicio Militar Nacional (National Military Service definition), Ministry of National Defense website, available from *www.sedena.gob.mx/index.php/servicio-militar-nacional.*

34. Inigo Guevara Moyano, "Mexican anti-drug conscripts complete first tour," *Jane's Defence Weekly*, August 7, 2009 .

35. Ministry of National Defense, *Fourth Annual Report (2006-2012)*, p. 128.

36. Francisco Garfias, "Narco para rato" (*"Narco for a long time"*), *Excelsior Newspaper*, October 6, 2010, available from *excelsior.com.mx/index.php?m=nota&id_nota=669731.*

37. "PRI surprised due to budget cuts to Ministry of National Defense," *El Informador*, November 18, 2010, available from *www.informador.com.mx/mexico/2010/249878/6/sorprende-al-pri-recortes-en-la-sedena.htm* .

38. The UN Conventional arms register considers conventional weapons as being combat aircraft, attack helicopters, tanks, armored vehicles, artillery pieces over 75 mm in caliber, submarines, and naval vessels over 500 tons in displacement.

39. Ministry of National Defense, "Estudio de Costo-Eficiencia, Programa de Adquisición de equipos de radio" ("Cost-Efficiency Study: Radio Equipment Acquisition Program"), p. 5.

40. Ministry of National Defense, "Documento de Analisis Costo-Eficiencia, Programa de Adquisición de Vehículos Ligeros para transporte de personal" ("Cost-Efficiency Study: Light Vehicle Personnel Transport Acquisition Program"), p. 5.

41. Ministry of National Defense, *Fourth Annual Report (2009-2010)*, pp. 62, 75.

42. Andres Merslo and Juan Arvizu Eroga, SEDENA, "4,600 mdp para equipo anticrimen" ("4,600 million pesos for anti-crime equipment"), available from *www.eluniversal.com.mx/nacion/183852.html.*

43. SHCP Cartea de programas y Proyectos de inversión (Ministry of Finance, Investment Project and Programs Portfolio), No.10071170002.

44. Ministry of National Defense, *Fourth Annual Report (2009-2010)*, p. 95.

45. Eight Bell 412EP helicopters were transferred under the Merida Initiative; the rest include five C-295Ms, five C-130Hs, and 50 Bell 206B/Ls transferred from PGR, and 12 EC725s.

46. Ministry of National Defense-IFAI, July 2010 Information Requirement, available from *www.sedena.gob.mx/pdf/ifai/2010/julio_2010.pdf.*

47. SHCP Carpeta de Programas y Proyectos de Inversión (Ministry of Finance, Investment Project and Programs Portfolio), No. 07071320002.

48. Nicolas Lucas, "Queretaro apuntado para recibir a Eurocopter" ("Queretaro aims to obain Eurocopter plant"), *El Financiero*, January 14, 2011.

49. Ministry of National Defense, *Second Annual Report (2007-2008)*, p. 92.

50. Ministry of National Defense, *Fourth Annual Report (2009-2010)*, p. 95.

51. "Estrechan Colombia y Mexico cooperación de lucha antidrogas" ("Colombia and Mexico tighten anti-drug cooperation"), December 26, 2010, available from *www.radioformula.com.mx/notas.asp?Idn=147756.*

52. Ministry of National Defense, *First Annual Report (2006-2007)*, p. 75.

53. Jorge Luis Sierra, "La degradación de la fuerza militar" ("The degradation of military force"), *El Universal*, December 3, 2008, available from *www.eluniversal.com.mx/editoriales/42272.htm.*

54. Ministry of the Navy, Acuerdo Secretarial No. 87 (Secretarial Agreement No. 87), June 1, 2007.

55. Explanation of motives for the decree that reforms, adds, or derogates diverse dispositions that make up the Organic Law of the Mexican Navy.

56. Refers to vessels able to project power regionally.

57. Ministry of the Navy, Project 09132110001, Construcción de dos Buques de Aprovisionamiento Logístico, Cascos 42 y 4 (Construction of two Logistics Supply Vessels), July 2010.

58. Inigo Guevara Moyano, *A Full Throttle Future, Warships – International Fleet Review*, East Sussex, UK: HPC Publishing, February 2008, p. 19.

59. Dockstavarvet CB90 model webpage, available from *www. dockstavarvet.se/Products/Combat_patrol_boats/CB_90_H/Models. aspx*.

60. Dockstavarvet IC16M model webpage, available from *www.dockstavarvet.se/Products/Combat_patrol_boats/IC_16_M.aspx*.

61. Jesus Aranda, "'Desastroso' alistamiento de marinos en la PFP; sufrieron 'doble traición'" ("'Disastrous' recruitment of marines in Federal Police: they suffered 'double treason'," *La Jornada*, December 30, 2006.

62. Ministry of the Navy, Secretarial Agreement No. 88, June 1, 2007.

63. Ministry of the Navy, Project 10132160001, Adquisición de Aviones Versión Transporte Militar y Carga (Acquisition of Military Transport and Cargo Aircraft Program), June 2010, p. 5.

64. *Ibid.*

65. Ministry of the Navy, Programa de inversión de adquisiciones Adquisición de un Sistema de Vigilancia Aérea No Tripulado (Investment Program: Acquisition of an Unmanned Aircraft System), July 2009.

www.ingramcontent.com/pod-product-compliance
Lightning Source LLC
Chambersburg PA
CBHW060008300526
45794CB00003B/1136